ARACHNID WORLD

ORB WEAVERS

SANDRA MARKLE

HUNGRY SPINNERS

L LERNER PUBLICATIONS COMPANY MINNEAPOLIS

FOR CURIOUS KIDS EVERYWHERE

ACKNOWLEDGMENTS

The author would like to thank Dr. Todd Blackledge, University of Akron; and Dr. Simon Pollard, Canterbury Museum, Christchurch, New Zealand, for sharing their expertise and enthusiasm. A special thanks to Skip Jeffery for his support during the creation of this book.

Lerner Publications Company
A division of Lerner Publishing Group, Inc.
241 First Avenue North
Minneapolis, MN 55401 U.S.A.

Website address: www.lernerbooks.com

Library of Congress Cataloging-in-Publication Data

Markle, Sandra.
    Orb weavers : hungry spinners / by Sandra Markle.
        p.   cm. — (Arachnid world)
    Includes bibliographical references and index.
    ISBN 978–0–7613–5039–2 (lib. bdg. : alk. paper)
    ℐ. Orb weavers—Juvenile literature. I. Title.
    QL458.42.A7M37 2011
    595.4'4—dc22   2010023490

Manufactured in the United States of America
1 - DP - 12/31/10

10/11

CONTENTS

AN ARACHNID'S WORLD

WELCOME TO THE WORLD OF ARACHNIDS

(ah-RACK-nidz). Arachnids can be found in every habitat on Earth except in the deep ocean.

So how can you tell if an animal is an arachnid rather than a relative like an insect? Both belong to a group of animals called arthropods (AR-throh-podz). The animals in this group share some traits. They have bodies divided into segments, jointed legs, and a stiff exoskeleton. This is a skeleton on the outside like a suit of armor. One way that usually works to tell if an animal is an arachnid is to count its legs and body parts. While not every adult arachnid has eight legs, most do. Arachnids also usually have two main body parts. Most adult insects, like this horsefly (*right*), have six legs and three body parts.

This book is about orb-weaver spiders. All spiders produce silk. An orb weaver produces seven different kinds of silk. It can combine several kinds to build an orb-shaped (circular) web. Strong, tough, and beautiful, this web is an excellent trap for flying insects. The picture to the right shows a cross spider's orb web. Orb weavers usually hang head down in their webs.

ORB WEAVER FACT

An orb weaver's body temperature rises and falls with the temperature around it. So it must warm up to be active.

ON THE OUTSIDE

There are about three thousand different kinds of orb-weaver spiders. They all have two main body parts: the cephalothorax (sef-uh-loh-THOR-ax) and the abdomen. A tiny waistlike bit called the pedicel joins the two. The exoskeleton is made up of many plates connected by stretchy tissue. These let the spider bend and move. Take a close look at this female cucumber spider to discover other key features these spiders share.

EYES: These organs detect light and send messages to the brain for sight. Orb weavers have eight eyes. The large central eyes help the spider locate and catch insects for food. The smaller side eyes only see movement.

CHELICERAE (KEH-liss-ee-ray): These are a pair of jawlike mouthparts. They include fangs to stab insects and inject a poison liquid called venom.

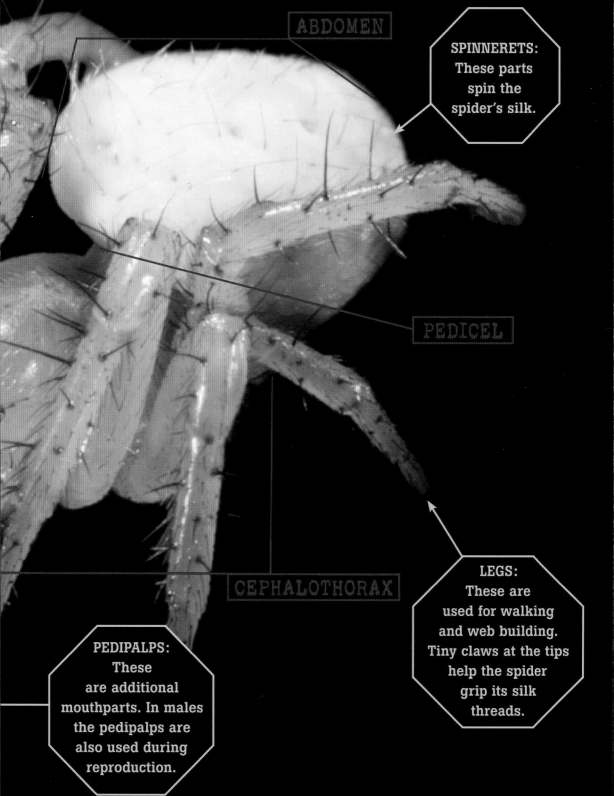

ABDOMEN

SPINNERETS:
These parts
spin the
spider's silk.

PEDICEL

CEPHALOTHORAX

LEGS:
These are
used for walking
and web building.
Tiny claws at the tips
help the spider
grip its silk
threads.

PEDIPALPS:
These
are additional
mouthparts. In males
the pedipalps are
also used during
reproduction.

ON THE INSIDE

Look inside an adult female orb weaver.

BRAIN: The brain receives messages from body parts and sends signals back to them.

SUCKING STOMACH: The stomach works with the pharynx to move food between the mouth and the gut.

VENOM GLAND: This body part produces venom.

PHARYNX (FAR-inks): This muscular tube pumps food into the stomach. Hairs in it also help filter out solid bits.

COXAL GLANDS: These are special groups of cells. They collect liquid wastes and pass them through openings to the outside of the body.

TRACHEAE: These tubes let air enter through holes called spiracles. Tracheae spread oxygen throughout the spider's body.

CAECA: These tubes store food.

Approved by Dr. Simon Pollard, Canterbury Museum, Christchurch, New Zealand

GUT: The body part that lets food nutrients pass into the blood.

HEART: This muscular tube pumps blood toward the head. The blood flows throughout the body and returns to the heart.

MALPIGHIAN (mal-PIG-ee-an) TUBULES: This system of tubes cleans the blood of wastes and dumps them into the gut.

OVARY: This organ produces eggs.

STERCORAL (STER-kor-ul) POCKET: Wastes collect here before passing out of the body.

SILK GLAND: This body part produces silk.

BOOK LUNGS: Blood circulates through these thin, flat folds of tissue. Air enters through the lung slits and passes into the spider's blood. Waste carbon dioxide gas exits through the book lungs.

SPERMATHECA (spur-muh-THEE-kuh): The female spider stores sperm in this sac after mating.

NERVE GANGLIA: These bundles of nerve tissue send messages between the brain and other body parts.

BECOMING ADULTS

Like all arachnids, orb-weaver spiders become adults through incomplete metamorphosis (me-teh-MOR-feh-sus). *Metamorphosis* means "change." An orb weaver's life includes three stages: egg, nymph or spiderling, and adult. Newly hatched spiderlings are blind and unable to eat. They stay in their egg sac until they molt, or shed their skin. Then they can see, and they begin to eat. They chew their way out of the egg sac and leave their siblings to live alone.

Compare these black-and-yellow garden spiderlings to the adult. The spiderlings have colorings and markings that are different too. Even so, they can do anything adults can do except mate and produce young.

SOME KINDS OF ARTHROPODS GO THROUGH COMPLETE METAMORPHOSIS. The four stages are egg, larva, pupa, and adult. Each stage looks and behaves very differently.

BLACK-AND-YELLOW GARDEN SPIDERLINGS

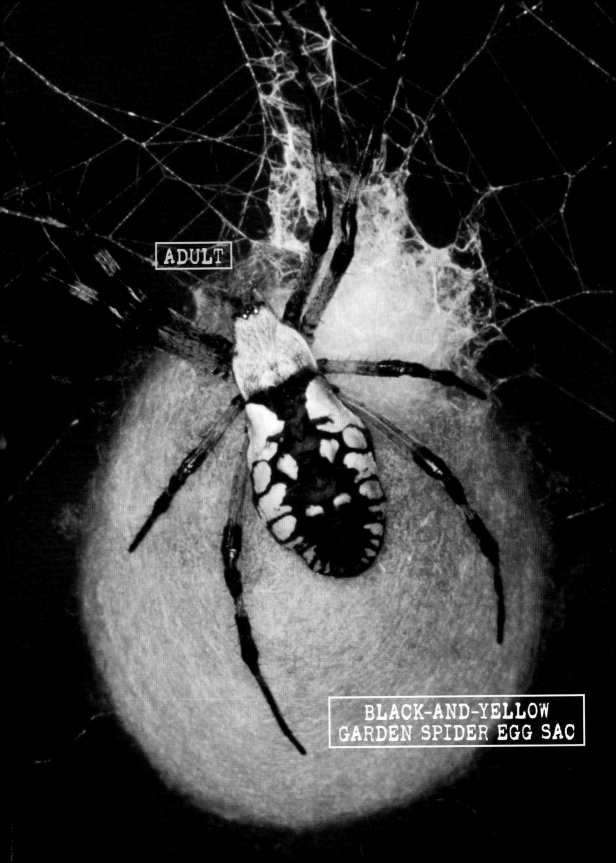

ADULT

BLACK-AND-YELLOW
GARDEN SPIDER EGG SAC

SPINNING FOR A LIVING

The focus of an orb weaver's life is catching insects to eat. But there are lots of spiders hunting for insects, so orb weavers do something special. They build midair snares—webs—to trap and hold flying insects.

The bodies of orb weavers produce seven different kinds of silk. They use just the right mix of dry and sticky silk strands to build their web snare. The golden orb weaver on the facing page has caught a butterfly.

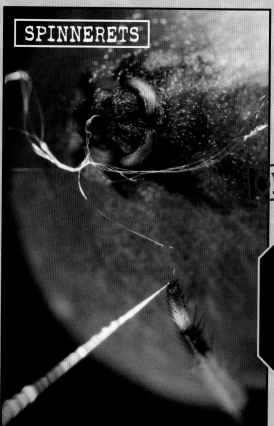

SPINNERETS

ORB WEAVER FACT

A spider's silk comes from nozzlelike parts called the spinnerets. Silk starts as a gooey liquid. It becomes a solid strand when the spider fastens it to something—even its own leg—and pulls.

Each type of orb weaver uses a slightly different web design. But like this female cross spider, each goes through the same basic web-building steps.

The orb weaver uses the distance between the tips of its back legs to its spinnerets for measuring the distances between strands. When the spider walks across its web, it can easily step from strand to strand.

First, the cross spider builds the web's frame with its strongest kind of silk. It is called dragline silk. Once the first strand is attached at each end, it walks over that strand, adding a second strand. It may even add more strands to make the web's main support extra strong. Then it spins the rest of the outside frame.

Next, the spider uses more dragline silk to form a *Y* across the framework. This creates the web's center. The spider spins more strong silk strands from the center like the spokes on a bicycle's wheel. The spider also adds about five strands circling the center point. That forms the web's hub.

To make the web a snare, the spider first spins a spiral of dry silk *(bottom)*. This silk spiral will act like a frame for the spider's final web building.

The orb weaver follows the dry silk spiral, and once again, it spins as it travels. This time, though, the strands the spider makes are coated with glue droplets. As the spider builds the new spiral of sticky silk, it bites out and eats the dry silk. Silk takes energy to make. By eating the unneeded silk, the spider gains some of the energy it needs for its web building.

The sticky silk strands make the web a trap. They catch the flying insects that touch them. The sticky strands are also elastic. They stretch rather than snap when an insect slams into them. That means that most insects are not able to break free once they are captured.

GARDEN SPIDER WALKING ON WEB

Like artists signing their work, some kinds of orb weavers finish their webs with special touches. Some add bands of nonsticky silk called stabilimenta (sta-bil-ee-MEN-tuh). Scientists aren't sure why spiders spin these. Stabilimenta may help the spider hide. Or they stop birds from flying into the web and damaging it. Stabilimenta may even attract insects.

The black-and-yellow garden spider is sometimes called a writing spider because of its zigzag stabilimentum. The silver argiope (r-GUY-oh-pee) builds a disk-shaped stabilimentum. The variable decoy spider takes a different approach. It uses silk to decorate its web with a string of garbage. The string may contain the remains of silk-wrapped insects, old egg sacs, and bits of leaves. When the spider climbs onto this line, it hides in plain sight.

ORB WEAVER FACT

Webs may be damaged. Sticky strands may become less sticky. So orb weavers regularly eat and rebuild their webs. Some do this job daily.

BLACK-AND-YELLOW GARDEN SPIDER

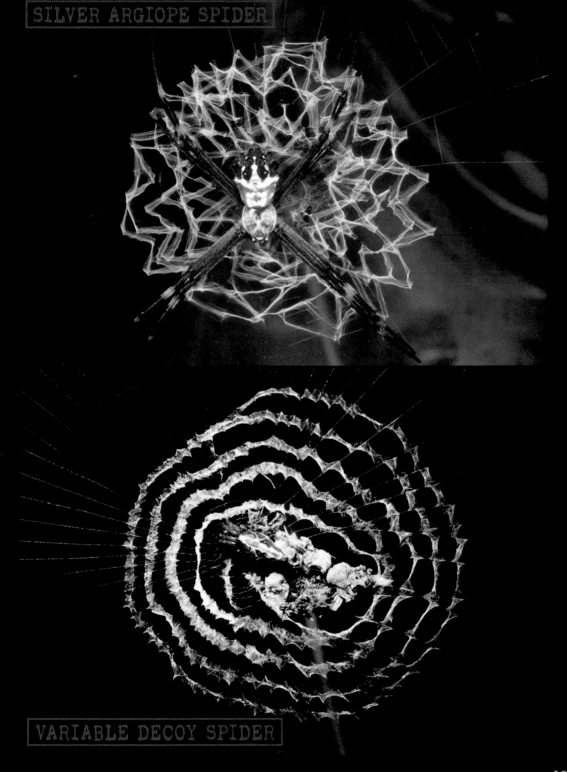

SILVER ARGIOPE SPIDER

VARIABLE DECOY SPIDER

19

CATCHING FAST FOOD

It's late summer and a storm rages. Fierce winds claw at the female cross spider's web. Wind-driven raindrops batter it. All the while, the spider stays safe on a nearby branch under a bit of loose bark. Finally, as daylight fades, the weather clears. The female cross spider crawls out of her hiding place. She goes to work, repairing her orb web. She removes the tattered spiral in the center and any broken outside lines. She eats the strands she removes. Then she starts spinning.

The female cross spider always builds the same web design. The remodeled web looks just like the original. She crosses her web walking on the nonsticky radials. Then she settles, head down, on the web's hub with her legs spread out. In this position, she touches and can check on most of the web's main strands.

ORB WEAVER FACT

The cross spider gets its name from the crosslike pattern of white dots on its abdomen.

The female cross spider's hard exoskeleton has lots of slits. Each of these openings exposes special sensory cells. When a fly zipping through the air strikes the spider's web, the silk strands stretch and spring back. Like a snapped rubber band, these movements shoot along strands. The spider senses these movements through the leg touching that web section. In an instant, the female cross spider is running toward the trapped insect. She keeps to the dry radial lines and steps over the sticky spiraling traplines.

As the fly tries to pull free, its efforts cause more of its body parts to touch sticky strands. It becomes even more firmly stuck. Its struggles create more such movements, and the spider tracks these to the fly.

ORB WEAVER FACT

An orb-weaver's sticky traplines are tougher than Kevlar, the fabric used to make bulletproof vests.

STRAINING DINNER

As soon as the female cross spider reaches the fly, she shoots bands of silk over it. She keeps on spinning while her feet turn the fly around and around.

Wrapped up, the fly can't escape. And it can't easily bite and injure her. The female cross spider sinks her fangs through the silk and injects a dose of venom (liquid poison) into the fly. This quickly quiets the insect. Then the spider tugs the wrapped fly toward the web's hub. There, she'll be harder for a hungry bird flying past to spot.

FANG

Once on her web hub, the female cross spider anchors the insect with a silk line and starts to eat. But like all spiders, she has a very small mouth. And like all arthropods, the fly has a hard exoskeleton. So the spider's first bite breaks open the fly's armor. Then she throws up digestive juices onto the fly's exposed soft body parts. Within seconds, the juices turn them into a liquid. The spider sucks in this food. She throws up more digestive juices and repeats the process. At the end of the meal, all that's left of the fly is its hard exoskeleton. The cross spider cuts the anchor line and lets this garbage drop out of her web.

With her meal over, the spider settles down to keep track of her web strands again *(right)*. And she stays alert for more movement—a signal her web has snared more food.

ORB WEAVER FACT

As the spider sucks in, its food flows through a screenlike plate *(right)*. Only liquid can pass through the tiny holes. Hard bits are trapped. The spider throws up these wastes to get rid of them.

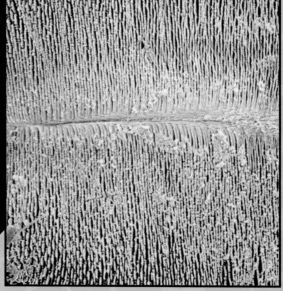

MATING SIGNALS

Hours later, the female cross spider detects movements again. But these are not random tugs made by a struggling insect. Her web strands are being plucked. It's a signal from a male cross spider looking for a mate.

Yesterday, just before the storm, the female cross spider molted for the last time. At that point, she became a mature adult female. As she spun to repair her storm-damaged web, she gave off pheromones (FAIR-eh-mohnz). These are special chemical signals. Like sniffing perfume, a male cross spider living nearby sensed these and tracked them to find her. He signals he's not something to eat by plucking her web strands. When she doesn't attack, he walks across her web toward her. He carries a small amount of sperm (male reproductive cells) on his paddle-shaped pedipalps. He inserts the sperm into her gonopore.

ORB WEAVER FACT

Like most spiders, the male cross spider is about half the size of the female. A female's body is about 0.7 inches (1.8 centimeters) long. The male's is about 0.35 inches (0.9 cm) long.

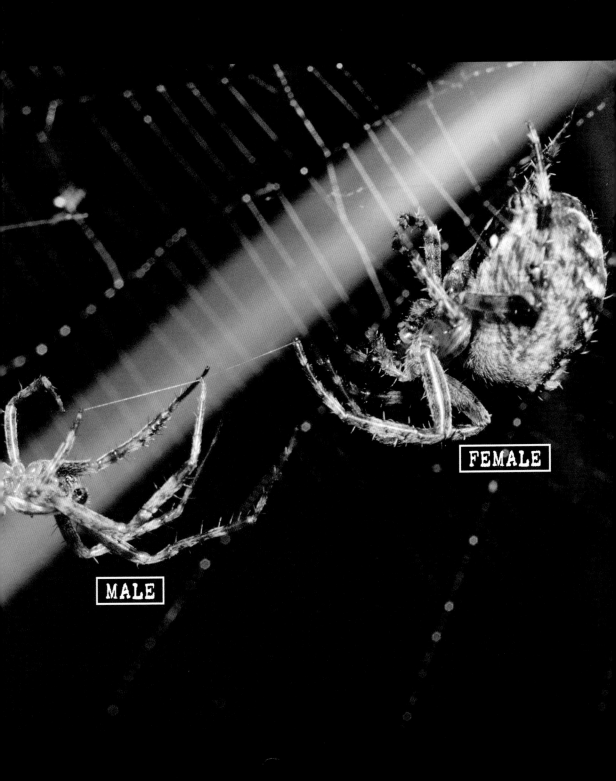

FEMALE

MALE

EGGS IN A SAC

After mating, the male leaves the female's web. He dies a short time later. After resting for a few days, the female starts to spin a silk disk. Onto this she deposits eggs, one at a time. As each egg cell leaves her body, it passes the stored sperm. When a sperm joins with an egg's cell, the egg develops a tough coat. Inside, a baby spider starts to grow.

As the female lays her eggs, she coats them with a sticky liquid to glue them together. She wraps the egg mass in more silk strands to create an egg sac. She goes on to make more eggs and sacs. So, if something happens to one egg sac, the rest are likely to remain safe.

The female only guards her egg sacs for a few days. Then she abandons them and dies. However, she has built her egg sacs in a sheltered spot so they are well hidden. They are likely to stay safe from hunting animals. The sacs are also tough enough to shelter the babies from bad weather.

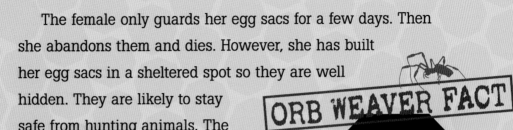

ORB WEAVER FACT

Female cross spiders usually lay from three hundred to eight hundred eggs.

EGGS IN EGG SAC

THE CYCLE CONTINUES

The baby cross spiders hatch. After a few weeks, they molt for the first time. They stay safely inside their egg sac all winter long. While the weather is cold, the spiderlings are quiet and don't eat. Once the weather warms up, they become active. They also chew on the egg sac wall. Their digestive juices help break down the tough silk. Finally, their effort creates an exit hole.

The spiderlings crawl out. They may remain together for another day or two. But so many spiderlings mean too many hunters in one place. Soon each spiderling pulls a silk strand out of its spinneret. When the wind catches this strand, the spiderling becomes airborne.

ORB WEAVER FACT

Hundreds of spiderlings may emerge from one egg sac. So a spiderling's first meal may be a weaker brother or sister.

A female cross spiderling goes where the wind carries her. When she lands, she searches for a spot to spin a web. Because the spiderling uses her legs as a measuring tool, her first web is little. It catches small insects. But eating gives her energy to grow. Soon her exoskeleton is too tight, and she has to molt again.

She attaches a silk line to her web. Then she drops down on it. Her hard, old exoskeleton breaks open. Her body separates from it. Slowly, the spiderling tugs and pulls her body and legs free. She waits while her new, bigger exoskeleton hardens.

The female spiderling continues to eat, grow, and molt as many as a dozen times before she becomes a mature adult. Each time she molts, she's bigger than before. As she grows bigger, she builds larger webs to catch larger meals.

ORB WEAVER FACT

Each time an orb weaver molts, it develops more of the adult colorings and markings.

By late summer, the female is ready to molt one last time. As in past molts, she is already covered by her new exoskeleton. What's different this time is that she's become a mature adult. She is ready to mate and produce young.

So a day later, as she spins to repair her web, she coats the strands with pheromones. Nearby, a male cross spider has become an adult too. He no longer builds webs to catch insects. Instead, he wanders, searching for a mate. Tracking the female's chemical signals, he finds the female in her web. Then they mate.

ORB WEAVER FACT

As long as a spiderling is growing and molting, it can regenerate, or regrow, a lost part, such as a leg. The new part develops folded up inside the injury site. It unfolds during the next molt.

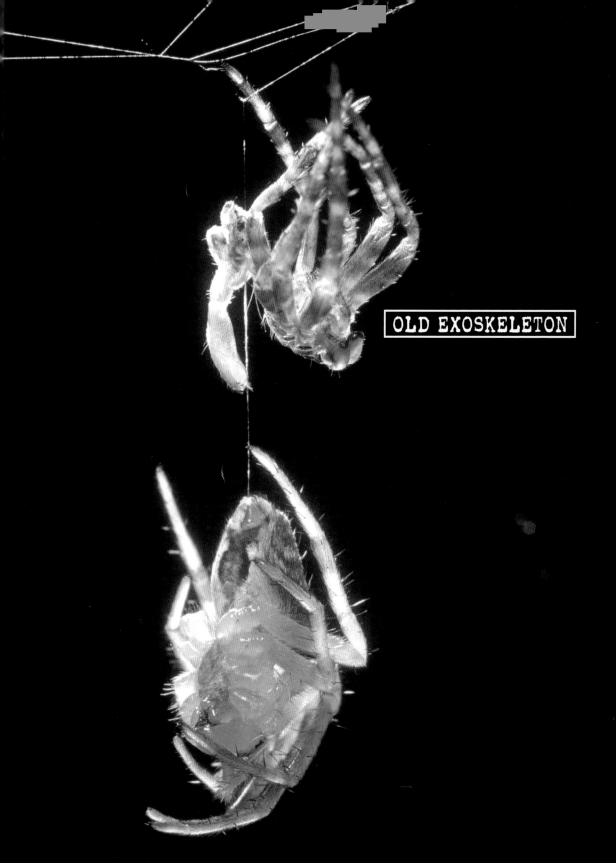

OLD EXOSKELETON

Only a few of each kind of orb weaver live long enough to grow up and mate. Most become targets for birds and other hunting animals. Those that become adults, like this female cross spider, are able to spin the biggest webs of their lives. Each web trap the female cross spider builds is nearly 16 inches (40 cm) across. She is able to catch big insects too, such as this wasp. This big meal gives her an energy boost. That's the energy she needs to produce eggs and build egg sacs. Generation after generation, the cycle of an orb-spinning life continues.

ORB WEAVERS AND OTHER TRAP-BUILDING SPIDERS

Orb weavers belong to a group, or order, of arachnids called Araneae (ah-RAN-ee-eye). These are the spider members of the arachnid group. Most orb weavers belong to a family of spiders, the Araneidae (ah-RAN-ee-day). There are about three thousand different kinds worldwide. They all build circular webs that are much bigger than they are. These large webs give them a larger area in which to catch insects than they could otherwise reach. Scientists group living and extinct animals with others that are similar. So orb weavers are classified this way:

kingdom: Animalia
phylum: Arthropoda
class: Arachnida
order: Araneae
family: Araneidae

HELPFUL OR HARMFUL? Orb weavers are both, but they're mainly helpful because they eat a lot of insects. They help control insect populations that could otherwise become pests. They're harmful because, while they only bite in self-defense, their bite does inject venom. Their venom isn't generally harmful to people, but some people might have an allergic reaction to it.

HOW BIG IS an orb weaver? A female cross spider's body is about 0.7 inches (1.8 cm) long. A male's is only about 0.35 inches (0.9 cm) long.

MORE TRAP-BUILDING SPIDERS

Spiders are the only trap-building arachnids. But orb weavers aren't the only spiders that build a trap to catch a meal. Compare the traps built by these spiders to the one designed by an orb weaver.

Bowl and doily spiders build two webs, one above the other. The

lower web is a horizontal sheet web, the doily. The upper web is bowl shaped. The spider hangs upside down from its bowl web. It's a tiny spider (only about 0.2 inches, or 4 millimeters) long. But its web gives it a big advantage. When flies, gnats, or other insects drop into the bowl-shaped web, the spider rushes to that spot and bites through the web strands. The insect drops onto the doily. It is trapped between the two webs, giving the spider time to attack and wrap up its meal.

Trapdoor spiders use their silk to spin a door for a burrow they dig

into the ground. The spider hides inside the burrow. It holds the door half open, gripping it with the claws on its feet. It waits there until it senses movements that mean an insect is moving nearby. Then it throws open the trapdoor and charges out to attack and capture its meal.

GLOSSARY

abdomen: the back end of an arachnid, which contains systems for digestion, reproduction, and silk production

adult: the final, reproductive stage of an arachnid's life cycle

book lungs: thin, flat folds of tissue where blood circulates

brain: this organ receives messages from sense organs and other body parts and sends signals to control them

caeca: branching tubes through which the liquid food passes and where food is stored

cephalothorax: the front end of an arachnid, where the mouth, the brain, and the eyes are located. Legs are also attached to the cephalothorax.

chelicerae: a pair of jawlike parts that end in fangs. Spiders use the fangs to stab insects and inject venom.

coxal glands: special groups of cells for collecting liquid wastes and ridding the spider of them through an opening to the outside

egg: a female reproductive cell; also the name given to the first stage of an arachnid's life cycle

exoskeleton: the protective, armorlike skeleton on the outside of an arachnid's body

eyes: sensory organs that detect light and send signals to the brain for sight

fangs: a pair of toothlike parts of the spider's chelicerae. A liquid poison called venom flows out of the fang through a hole near the tip.

gut: the body part that sends food nutrients into the blood that are then carried throughout the body

heart: the muscular tube that pumps blood forward. Then the blood flows throughout the body and back to the heart.

Malpighian tubules: a system of tubes that cleans the blood of wastes and dumps them into the intestine

molt: the process of an arachnid shedding its exoskeleton

nerve ganglia: bundles of nerve tissue that send messages between the brain and other body parts

ovary: the body part that produces eggs

pedicel: the waistlike part in spiders that connects the cephalothorax to the abdomen

pedipalps: a pair of leglike body parts that extend from the head near the mouth. They help catch an insect and hold it for eating.

pharynx: a muscular tube that expands and contracts to create a pump to pull food into the body's digestive system. Hairs in the pharynx help filter out any solid bits.

pheromones: chemicals given off as a form of communication

silk gland: the body part that produces silk

sperm: a male reproductive cell

spermatheca: a sac in female arachnids that stores sperm after mating

spiderling: the name given to the stage between egg and adult in spiders

spinnerets: the body part that spins silk

spiracle: the small opening in the exoskeleton that leads into the trachea

stercoral pocket: the place where wastes collect before passing out of the body

sucking stomach: a muscular stomach that along with the pharynx pulls liquid food into an arachnid's gut. Cells in the stomach lining produce digestive juices.

trachea: tubes that help spread oxygen throughout the spider's body. They also store oxygen.

venom gland: the body part that produces venom

DIGGING DEEPER

To keep on investigating orb web spiders, explore these books and online sites:

BOOKS

Allman, Toney. *From Spider Webs to Man-Made Silk*. San Diego: KidHaven Press, 2005. Find out why spider silk is useful. Then investigate how scientists have engineered a man-made silk that mimics its unique properties.

Markle, Sandra. *Sneaky Spinning Baby Spiders*. New York: Walker Books for Young Readers, 2008. Compare how orb-weaver spiderlings hatch and grow up to the life cycles of other kinds of spiders.

Robinson, W. Wright. *Animal Architects: How Spiders and Other Silkmakers Build Their Amazing Homes*. San Diego: Blackirch Press, 1999. Compare how the orb weavers build their webs to the way other animals make and use silk.

Singer, Marilyn. *Venom*. Minneapolis: Millbrook Press, 2007. Find out about creatures that can harm or even kill with a bite or a sting.

Souza, D. M., *Packed with Poison!* Minneapolis: Millbrook Press, 2006. Learn about the most venomous and poisonous animals in the world.

MORE FROM SANDRA MARKLE

INSECT WORLD:
Diving Beetles
Hornets
Locusts
Luna Moths
Mosquitoes
Praying Mantises
Stick Insects
Termites

WEBSITES

All about Spiders
http://www.coopext.colostate.edu/4DMG/Pests/spiders.htm
Check out facts and photos about spiders commonly found in North
American gardens, including orb weaver spiders. Discover how to
encourage spiders to live in your garden and why you want them there.

An Ancient Spider's Web
http://www.sciencenewsforkids.org/articles/20060628/Note3.asp
Find out about the discovery of a spider and part of its web in
110-million-year-old amber (fossilized tree sap).

How Spiders Catch His Prey
http://www.youtube.com/watch?v=2VWLYy4vyso&NR=1
Watch a spider catch its food on its web. Note: the title of this site says
"His" web, but it is most likely a female spider.

Spider Fact Index
http://www.kidzone.ws/lw/
spiders/facts.htm
This site is packed with
interesting spider facts and
photos. Don't miss the "Activities"
section of this site.

LERNER SOURCE

Visit www.lerneresource.com
**for free, downloadable arachnid
diagrams, research assignments
to use with this series, and
additional information about
arachnid scientific names.**

ORB WEAVER ACTIVITY

An orb weaver only has to guard a few main web threads to sense where there's activity. Then it can move in that direction. Follow these steps to get a feel for how spiders get information from their webs.

1. Collect three rubber bands that are about the same length and thickness.

2. Hold your hands in front of you, palm sides together.

3. Have a partner hook one rubber band over your two index fingers. Then have your partner hook the second and third rubber bands over the next two pairs of fingers.

4. Move your hands just far enough apart to stretch the rubber bands slightly. These are like the elastic strands of sticky silk in an orb weaver's web.

5. Close your eyes. Then have your partner gently pluck one of the rubber bands. Try to tell which rubber band was plucked. Repeat several times. Have your partner pluck gently and then harder. See if you can tell the difference.

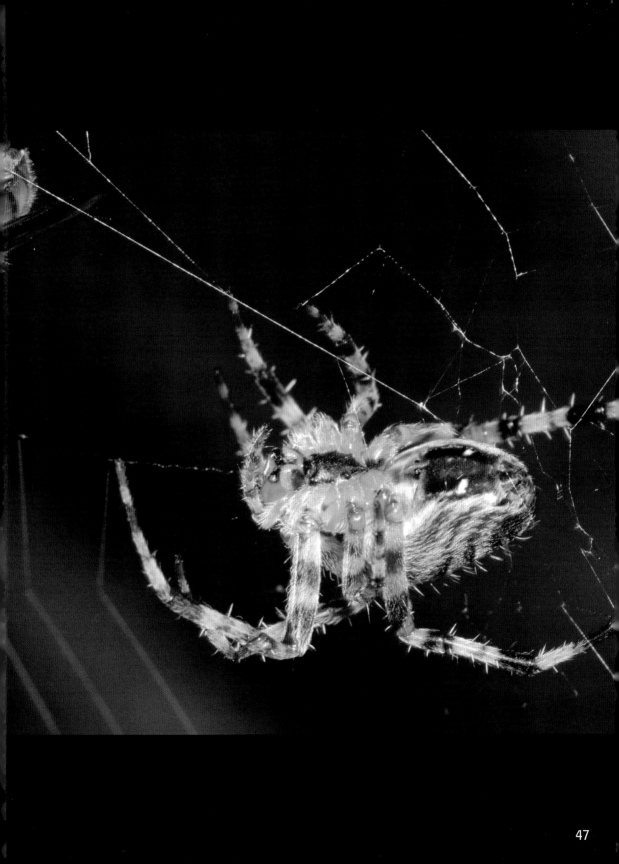

INDEX

PHOTO ACKNOWLEDGMENTS

The images in this book are used with the permission of: © Duncan McEwan/naturepl.com, p. 4; © Wolfgang Kaehler, www.wkaehlerphoto.com, p. 5; © Kim Taylor/naturepl.com, pp. 6–7; © Perennou Nuridsany/Photo Researchers, Inc., p. 6 (inset); © Dwight Kuhn, p. 10; © Reinhold, Ralph/Animals Animals, p. 11; © Stephen Dalton/naturepl.com, p. 12; © Ray Coleman/Visuals Unlimited, Inc., p. 13; © Christina Bollen/Oxford Scientific/Photolibrary, p. 14; © OSF/Cooke, J.A.L./ Animals Animals, pp. 15, 16 (bottom), 25; © Andrew Syred/Photo Researchers, Inc., p. 16 (top); © WILD & NATURAL/Animals Animals, p. 17; © Segars, Herb/Animals Animals, p. 18; © Gerry Bishop/Visuals Unlimited, Inc., p. 19 (top); © Premaphotos/naturepl.com, pp. 19 (bottom), 28–29; © Stephen Dalton/Minden Pictures, p. 21; © Jef Meul/Minden Pictures, pp. 22–23, 46–47; © Meul/ ARCO/naturepl.com, pp. 24, 35; © Bruce Cutler, p. 26; © Paulo De Oliveira/Photolibrary/Getty Images, p. 27; © Laurie Campbell/NHPA/Photoshot, p. 30; © OSF/Watts, B./Animals Animals, p. 31; © Michael Durham/www.DurmPhoto.com, pp. 32–33; © Robert Noonan/Photo Researchers, Inc., p. 37; © Marko König/imagebroker.net/Photolibrary, pp. 38–39; © John Shaw/NHPA/Photoshot, p. 41 (top); © Hans Christoph Kappel/naturepl.com, p. 41 (bottom). Illustrations by © Independent Picture Service.

Front cover: © Derrick Hamrick/imagebroker RF/Photolibrary.